To M.W. – S.K.
For Toby – T.T.

With thanks to Dr Mike Goldsmith
for casting his scientific eye over this book

Bloomsbury Publishing, London, Berlin and New York

First published in Great Britain in 2009 by Bloomsbury Publishing Plc
36 Soho Square, London, W1D 3QY

Text copyright © Tracey Turner 2009
Illustrations copyright © Sally Kindberg 2009

The moral rights of the author and illustrator have been asserted

A CIP catalogue record of this book is available from the British Library

ISBN 978 0 7475 9432 1

All papers used by Bloomsbury Publishing are natural, recyclable products
made from wood grown in well-managed forests. The manufacturing processes
conform to the environmental regulations of the country of origin.

Printed in Singapore

1 3 5 7 9 10 8 6 4 2

www.bloomsbury.com

the COMIC STRIP

ooh!

History

of

Space

Squeeak

Sally Kindberg
and Tracey Turner

BLOOMSBURY

Contents

Who knows? There are plenty of theories though...

Or, an all-powerful GOD created everything.
(There are many different versions of him/her/it.)

Then (probably)...

BIG BANG THEORY

In 1927, a priest called GEORGE LEMAÎTRE was studying astronomy...

Galaxies are whizzing along at alarming speeds...

I know!

Hmm... the UNIVERSE seems to be expanding!

There must have been a huge COSMIC EXPLOSION that started everything!

Wow!

At first...

Rubbish!

Pah!

What nonsense!

Piffle!

Silly billy!

But a few years later...

Of course

Brilliant.

Obvious when YOU think about it!

Excellent theory!

Now just about everyone accepts BIG BANG theory. It says...

About 13·7 billion years ago, all the matter in the Universe was SQUISHED into a very small space.

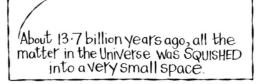

It was incredibly HOT

and incredibly DENSE. Lots of stuff—EVERYTHING actually—packed in here

Then it exploded, E–X–P–A–N–D–I–N–G outwards...

And then, about 300,000 years after the Big Bang...

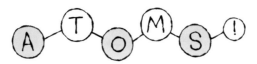

ATOMS!

The Universe cooled down enough for ATOMS to form.

The nuclei were a bit useless on their own, so they met up with electrons and became ATOMS.

Hi... I'm an ELECTRON.

And I'm irresistibly drawn to you.

We give things structure. Without us there wouldn't be any THINGS at all!

Ooh... I'd go weak at the knees if I had any!

And we allow LIGHT to travel. Without us everything would be DARK.

GULP!

I just love all this attention!

Now we're an ATOM!

EVERYTHING is made of atoms. Without atoms the Universe would be clouds of particles. and nothing else.

An ancient Greek called DEMoCRITUS was the first person to think about atoms.

Hmm...

Erm...

Everything's made up of really titchy things

...which are the smallest things there are!

I know! I'll call them άτομα *

* atoms

Apart from hydrogen and helium, nothing else existed until millions of years later...

A Star is born...

The Universe carried on COOLING, and GRAVITY pulled the hydrogen and helium closer together

WHOOSH WHOOSH

...causing NUCLEAR REACTIONS

...which created the first STARS (giant balls of burning GAS) ...and so the first GALAXIES were born.

There are about 100 BILLION stars in the MILKY WAY.

There are HUNDREDS of BILLIONS of galaxies in the Universe.

Some galaxies are SPIRALS, some are ELLIPSES, and some are just BLOBS.

The Milky Way, our galaxy, is a very attractive spiral.

I'm a BLOB and proud of it!

Long before our Sun existed, some of these first stars began to die ...

SUPERNOVAS

When a STAR has burned up all its hydrogen it starts to do this...

WHIZZ

FIZZ

BANG

NUCLEAR REACTION

But if it's VERY big, the dying star explodes as a SUPERNOVA...which can burn brighter than all the other stars in its galaxy put together

BANG

BANG

Small stars will expand to become RED GIANTS.

Heh heh

Not this kind and we've got the colour wrong anyway...

URK

The NUCLEAR REACTIONS and explosions make atoms fuse together to create new, different atoms...

The explosions scatter us throughout the Universe.

Whee!

A billion or so years after the Universe began, the first exploding stars meant that hydrogen and helium atoms at last had some new friends

Hello there!

I'm an oxygen atom

Lovely weather!

Complicated atoms... like URANIUM... are the results of many supernovas over millions of years.

The Sun

Long after the Big Bang, a huge cloud of hydrogen and helium was whizzing through space...

Whooshy WHOOSH

Dust and stuff in here too, made from other STARS.

Suddenly...

WHUMP!!!!

it was squished into a DISC.

Hmm... maybe because of a nearby supernova?

From the huge disc of gases our SUN was formed...

Like other stars, the Sun is a giant ball of burning hydrogen gas... It is the closest star to Earth.

Inside the Sun, NUCLEAR REACTIONS turn 240 tonnes of hydrogen into heat and light EVERY MINUTE

At its core, the temperature is around 15 MILLION° C!

Whew!!

Why? Why?

Hmm? hmm?

The Sun is more than a MILLION MILLION times bigger than the Earth.

Great gas bubbles pop out of the CORONA during SUN STORMS.

BLIP BLOP

The corona extends millions of kilometres out into space from the surface of the Sun. It's nowhere near as bright as the surface, yet it's millions of degrees HOTTER This puzzles scientists.

And, eventually, there was...

OUR SOLAR SYSTEM

Dwarf planets

The planets and moons that ORBIT our Sun formed 46 billion years ago.

Neptune

Uranus

Saturn

Hitch-hiking not recommended.

Jupiter

Asteroid Belt

Mars

Earth

Venus

Even though it speeds along, light still takes A DAY to cross our solar system.

Mercury

The Sun

MERCURY... is small and cratered.

The temperature varies a bit...430°C during the day

Whew

Brr...

...and –170°C at night.

The atmosphere is very thin. Radiation from the Sun is INTENSE!

SIZZLE SIZZLE

VENUS... is about the size of Earth and has huge volcanoes.

It's even HOTTER than Mercury (460°C) because the CARBON DIOXIDE atmosphere stores heat.

STINKY

The clouds are made of SULPHURIC ACID, and the pressure is 100 times Earth's. That's the bad news...

The good news is that, it can be your birthday and Christmas EVERY DAY of the year...

creak creak

as Venus spins slowly, so a DAY is longer than a YEAR on Earth.

EARTH...

All mod cons

Lots of WATER

PEOPLE and STUFF

(more on that later)

15

MARS

Deimos

CANYONS

Phobus

has the highest MOUNTAINS in the solar system.

People thought there might be LIFE on Mars...

Look! There's a canal system...

I hope the MARTIANs are friendly!

If there ever was life, it looked like this...

simple BACTERIA

and died out millions of years ago.

Little do you know, foolish earthlings!

Nng!

ASTEROID BELT

JUPITER...

GREAT RED SPOT

Jupiter's a GAS GIANT—as are Saturn, Uranus and Neptune

is absolutely HUGE... twice as HEAVY as all the other planets put together.

Jupiter is a giant ball of LIQUID and GAS (though there's a core of solid hydrogen).

SQUOOOSH!

An enormous HURRICANE has been raging away on Jupiter for more than 300 years (this is Jupiter's famous Great Red Spot).

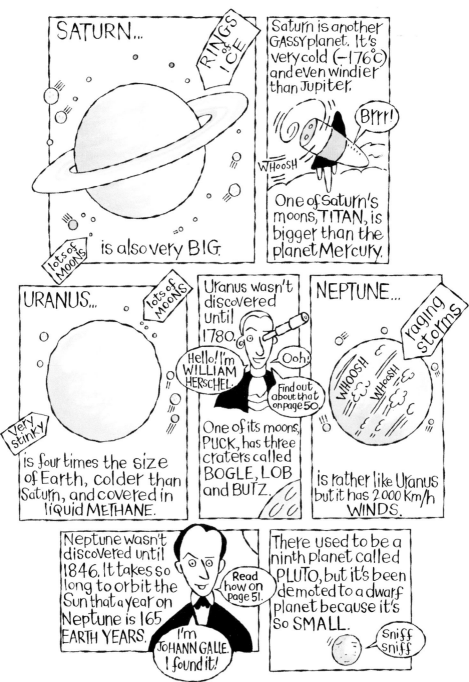

SATURN...

RINGS of ICE

is also very BIG.

lots of MOONS

Saturn is another GASSY planet. It's very cold (−176°C) and even windier than Jupiter.

Brrr!

WHOOSH

One of Saturn's moons, TITAN, is bigger than the planet Mercury.

URANUS...

lots of MOONS

Very stinky

is four times the size of Earth, colder than Saturn, and covered in liquid METHANE.

Uranus wasn't discovered until 1780.

Hello! I'm WILLIAM HERSCHEL.

Ooh!

Find out about that on page 50.

One of its moons, PUCK, has three craters called BOGLE, LOB and BUTZ.

NEPTUNE...

raging storms

WHOOSH WHOOSH

is rather like Uranus but it has 2,000 km/h WINDS.

Neptune wasn't discovered until 1846. It takes so long to orbit the Sun that a year on Neptune is 165 EARTH YEARS.

Read how on page 51.

I'm JOHANN GALLE. I found it!

There used to be a ninth planet called PLUTO, but it's been demoted to a dwarf planet because it's so SMALL.

Sniff sniff

PLANET EARTH

Whizzes through space, spinning around once every 24 hours or so...

Attractive blue colour because WATER covers nearly 75% of surface

Giant ball of solid NICKEL-IRON at centre

Earth's CRUST is a thin layer of ROCK

Thick layer of gases covers the planet – the ATMOSPHERE

Water is essential for life on Earth.

Nice day!

The atmosphere FILTERS some of the Sun's harmful RADIATION. It's also useful for BREATHING.

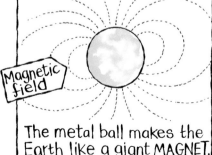

Magnetic field

The metal ball makes the Earth like a giant MAGNET. This is useful because it deflects harmful particles from the Sun.

Sections of the Earth's crust grind against each other, causing EARTHQUAKES and VOLCANOES.

CREAK   BIFF   BASH   BLIP

And even creating MOUNTAINS and CONTINENTS (which takes a while).

A few hundred
million years later
(no one knows
how or where)
ORGANISMS
appeared...

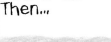

Then...

Later...

Later still...

There was bluey-green
ALGAE for about
3 billion years.

Then...

Until...

DINOSAURS were
around for 175
million years.

And we were nosier than the dinosaurs...

People had interesting ideas about what MIGHT be going on UP THERE...

But the Babylonians were the REAL smartypants...

THE ANCIENT BABYLONIANS

The BABYLONIANS were the first to name and number the stars and planets...

We can use our maths

to predict their movements!

Gosh, there's another one!

scritch scratch

scritch scratch

Babylonian clay tablets are the oldest astronomical records in the world.

They believed the stars and planets were ruled by GODS.

The Sun is called SHAMASH

...and that's planet NERGAL—the war god.

Ooh!

Later, the GREEKS and ROMANS used the same system as the Babylonians but replaced the Babylonian gods with their own.

I'm an ancient Roman and the planet Nergal is MARS, our own war god.

I'm a modern person, and now Mars is...er...still Mars.

What goes on up there affects what goes on down here on Earth.

So get praying!

HISS

Babylonian observatories were attached to temples.

The movements of the stars and planets were used to make predictions about people's lives.

Aha! Things are looking very promising for your reign, O king.

We also predicted the future using animals' LIVERS, by the way.

Oh, smashing!

Keep up the good work!

They also thought up names for the constellations...

27

Constellations

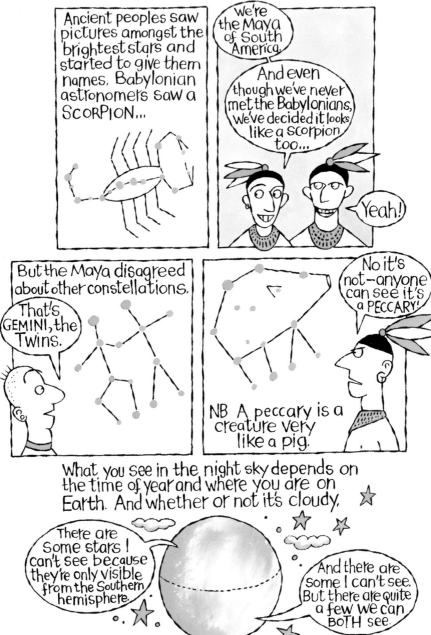

Ancient peoples weren't only interested in space by night...

Ancient Chinese Ideas

This is what happens in a
SOLAR ECLIPSE

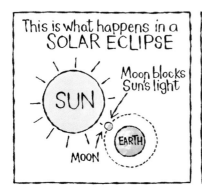

Moon blocks Sun's light

SUN

EARTH

MOON

and a LUNAR ECLIPSE.

SUN

EARTH

MOON

Earth's shadow falls on Moon

Solar eclipses are particularly dramatic.

Aargh

YOWL

URK

The first record of a total eclipse of the Sun was in 2136 BC in China.

Nnnn!

Pull yourself together and write it down!

Unfortunately, solar eclipses were seen as a very bad omen in China.

Oh no, a dragon's devouring the Sun!

No, a dog's eating it!

Whichever way you look at it, this can't be good!

WHIMPER

So Chinese astronomers/astrologers spent a lot of time trying to foretell when they would occur.

We'll all need to hide under our beds a week next Tuesday.

SIGH

Every sunrise, the ancient EGYPTIAN god RE was born.

Gurgle

By midday he was an adult.

By evening, he was old.

Creak

Behave!

Sss!

I want to stop you on your journey!

And at night he travelled through the underworld.

Many other Egyptian gods were seen in the stars.

Look, there's OSIRIS, god of the dead.

So it is!

The MILKY WAY is the goddess NUT giving birth to Re!

I say!

The night sky was divided into groups of STAR GODS travelling in boats.

This is fun!

Ancient Egyptian priests were also astronomers.

We can PREDICT things...

like the annual flooding of the NILE.

The flood was important, which made the priests important too.

The flood is coming!

It happens after the bright star SIRIUS rises before the Sun.

Isn't he clever!

From around 2000 BC, Egyptian astronomers recognised FIVE planets (which we know as Mercury, Venus, Mars, Jupiter and Saturn).

*SBG is bright tonight

Is that good or bad?

*Sbg was an ancient Egyptian name for Mercury.

Some Egyptian buildings were aligned with the stars.

But the ancient Greeks had some REALLY good ideas...

ANCIENT GREEK THOUGHTS

About 2,500 years ago...

Hello. I'm PYTHAGORUS and...

The Earth is a SPHERE.

Also:

And don't eat beans

Ahem.

My name's ANAXAGORAS

The Sun and stars are fiery stones.

Gosh!

Just call me PLATO. I lived between 428 and 348.

Planets move at a constant speed along circular paths *

* which isn't quite right actually.

I'm his student, ARISTOTLE

The Sun, Moon and planets revolve round Earth *

* which is completely wrong but an easy mistake.

In the ancient city of ALEXANDRIA...

I'm ARISTARCHUS of Samos and...

actually the Earth revolves round the Sun!

Pah!

Let's ignore him—for a millennium or two!

Aristarchus also worked out how far away the Sun and Moon are.

Hm...

DARK AGE ASTRONOMERS

In EUROPE, nobody bothered thinking about space much

All that maths and stuff...

Who cares?

Anyone for a rampage?

Learned works of civilised world go up in smoke.

At ALEXANDRIA, the great library was burned down.

In INDIA, BRAHMAGUPTA had some clever thoughts...

The Earth is a moving sphere.

The Moon is illuminated by the Sun.

Hmm

In POLYNESIA, people had become star experts to help them navigate thousands of kilometres by sea.

Follow that star!

In NORTH AMERICA, the ANASAZI people painted the bright supernova explosion they'd observed in the sky.

Good heavens!

And in CHINA...

We noticed this too!

Copernicus

Copernicus's universe...

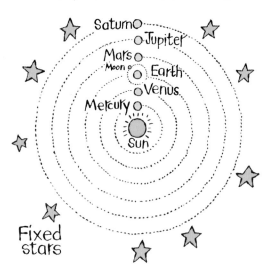

But Copernicus's calculations couldn't explain the way the planets moved...

Kepler, Brahe (and Moose)

Galileo

Huygens

Telescopes

Hubble has taken the most
detailed pictures of the most
distant objects in the Universe...

Pillars of Creation
in EAGLE NEBULA

SoMBRERO GALAXY

Cosmic Pearl round
an exploding star

CAT'S EYE NEBULA

Remains of supernova

KINDBERG GALAXY
(OK, I made that up. It's
a tea stain.)

The light from distant stars
takes so long to reach us
that we're looking BACK in
TIME.

Light from the CARINA
NEBULA takes 8000 years
to reach Earth, so we're
looking at it as it was
8000 years ago, during
our STONE AGE.

The HERSCHEL SPACE
OBSERVATORY is the
latest space
telescope.

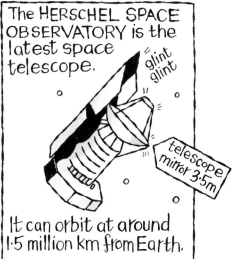

glint
glint

telescope
mirror 3.5m

It can orbit at around
1.5 million km from Earth.

Telescopes are useful, but it helps if you're a
bit of a boffin too...

And Newton had some clever chums...

COMETS!

EDMOND HALLEY was a mate of Newton's.

Yes, in fact I persuaded him to publish his work—he'd kept quiet about it for years!

Thanks, Ed!

He was also an astronomer.

I wrote a book about the southern stars.

In his spare time he made one of the first DIVING BELLS.

But he was most famous for...

COMETS are huge space snowballs made of ice, rock and metal.

As a comet travels closer to the Sun, it trails ice and dust behind it.

Comets orbit around the Sun in slightly WONKY paths.

Woe! Woe!

I'm the ancient Greek ARISTOTLE.

Comets cause STRONG WINDS and DROUGHT!

(they don't)

Comets were seen as a sign of DISASTER (which isn't true either—unless you're a DINOSAUR...)

urk

Halley used Newton's theories to work out that a particular comet returned close to the Earth at regular intervals.

Oh, no!

It appeared just before the BATTLE of HASTINGS in 1066.

Halley spotted it in 1682...

Hmm,... it has the same orbit as one that was last seen in 1607... it's the same one!

He didn't live to see it return as he'd predicted it would in 1758, by which time it had a name.

There goes Halley's Comet!

When Halley's Comet passed by in 1910, comet-protecting UMBRELLAS and anti-comet PILLS went on sale.

I say!

Some special comets...

Comet DONATI, seen in 1858, had 2 tails.

SHOEMAKER-LEVY 9 broke into bits and crashed into JUPITER in 1994.

HALE-BOPP, first seen in 1995, was especially big and bright.

Comet HYAKUTAKE had the longest tail ever — 570 million km (measured in 2000).

Comet-spotting became popular in the 1700s. Astronomer CAROLINE HERSCHEL discovered EIGHT of them.

There's another one!

One of them was named after her.

35P/HERSCHEL RIGOLLET

But Caroline wasn't as famous as her brother...

New Planets

WILLIAM HERSCHEL was a musician...

BOOMPA BOOMPA

and an astronomer in his spare time.

And he made telescopes, too...

It's a bit complicated, involves moulds using HORSE MANURE.

Pooh!

In 1781, with the help of his sister, the comet-hunter...

Ooh...I've discovered a new comet!

Another one?

YAWN

Hang on! It's not a comet, it's a new PLANET!

Yippee!

The other planets known about at this time (Mercury, Venus, Mars, Jupiter and Saturn) could all be seen with the naked eye.

After some debate, the new planet was called URANUS.

Uranus was the grandfather of Jupiter in classical mythology.

But I still prefer ROGER!

But as scientists delved further into space, our imaginations entered orbit as well...

SPACE STORIES

Back in 1668, MARGARET CAVENDISH wrote The Blazing World about a planet you can reach from the Arctic...

With some strange inhabitants,

Greetings, Parrot Man.

SQUARK!

Sss!

In a 1752 story by VOLTAIRE, a 120,000ft tall alien called MICROMEGAS...

travels to Earth on passing comets.

Hnn

In the space stories JULES VERNE wrote in the 1800s, three men are fired to the Moon by a cannon called Columbiad.

They orbit the Moon and make it back to Earth...

Whey-hey!

without meeting any aliens (not so different from what happened in 1968).

There have been hundreds of SPACE MOVIES...
Not many of them feature friendly aliens...

And plenty of TV series too...

At the start of the 20th century
in a Swiss patents office...

EINSTEIN

Meanwhile...

SPEEDING GALAXIES

The biggest TELESCOPE in the world was built on top of MOUNT WILSON in California.

I'm MILTON HUMASON.

Hmm, this looks interesting.

Can I have a go?

Humason got a job as a cleaner at Mount Wilson.

But it turned out he was a brilliant astronomer.

What an amazing supernova!

He's a natural!

Hello there!

Scientist EDWIN HUBBLE came to work at Mount Wilson. Together, they made some amazing discoveries.

A few years before...

I'm VESTO MELVIN SLIPHER.

I observed other GALAXIES that seemed to be moving away from us.

And I'm HENRIETTA LEAVITT. I discovered interesting things about the brightness of STARS.

Thanks to them and other astronomers

...we worked out the distances of other galaxies

...and how fast they're moving.

WHOOSH!

Meanwhile, in a galaxy far, far away...

Hubble and Humason had revealed the true vastness of the Universe.

But nobody knows much about planets in other solar systems within our own galaxy... let alone solar systems in other galaxies.

Hold on a bit, we're only just getting to know the ones in our own solar system.

The first planets outside our own solar system weren't discovered until 1992.

Hello, I'm ALEX WoLSZcZAN.

I found them!

300 or so planets have been proved to exist so far.

But within the visible Universe there are thought to be about 100 thousand million million million planets!

And if we don't know what they look like, how can we be sure they haven't arrived ALREADY...

There have been thousands of reports of UFOs.

That's an UNIDENTIFIED FLYING OBJECT.

YIKES!

LONELY HILL

Some of them remain a MYSTERY, and some people think they are the aircraft of ALIEN BEINGS.

Yoo hoo, Earthling!

We mean you no harm.

Heh heh

The most famous UFO incident happened in New Mexico.

Nothing... unusual... here... at... all...

We recovered a weather balloon near Roswell.

Hnn

It's a government cover-up!

They really recovered a crashed alien spacecraft

...and the dead bodies of real aliens!

urk

PRESS

Since then, there have been many reports of differently shaped UFOs, like this...

Or this...

But the only way to find out what's really out there is to go and check...

SPACE RACE

To get out of Earth's atmosphere and into space, you need a rocket...

The first ones were made in CHINA 1000 years ago and used as weapons.

Take that!

=WHOOSH

RUSSIAN scientist KONSTANTIN TsIOLKOVSKY was a rocket scientist

Whoosh!

Whoosh!

One day the human race will colonise space, live for ever and become perfect.

But he didn't actually launch one.

ROBERT GODDARD launched the first LIQUID-FUEL rocket in 1926...

WHOOSH

Wow... 12.5 metres

Well, it was a start.

GERMAN V-2 rockets were launched in 1942 as weapons in the Second World War.

Take that!

=WHOOSH

After the war, V-2s were developed for SPACE TRAVEL by a US team.

By this time, the two most powerful nations on Earth were the USA and USSR.

Yes, and we don't get on.

Nng

Nng

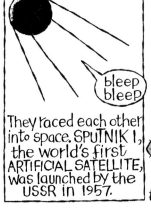

bleep bleep

They raced each other into space. SPUTNIK 1, the world's first ARTIFICIAL SATELLITE, was launched by the USSR in 1957.

The following year, the first US satellite, EXPLORER 1, was launched.

Whoosh

But we were first!

But going back to the start of the race...

But there have been some more unusual species too...

Croak

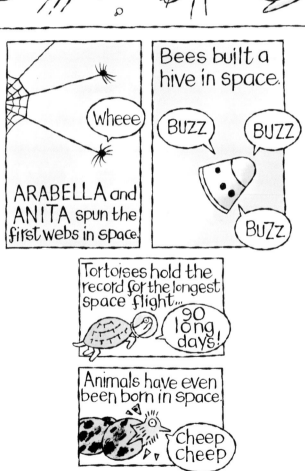

Wheee

ARABELLA and ANITA spun the first webs in space.

Bees built a hive in space.

BUZZ

BUZZ

BUZZ

Tortoises hold the record for the longest space flight...

90 long days!

Animals have even been born in space.

Cheep cheep

In 1961, the first PERSON went into space...

YURI GAGARIN

A 27-year-old Soviet pilot was about to become the most famous person on Earth...

I'm YURI!

Gosh!

On the way to the launch pad, Yuri had a pee (behind a bus). It's become a tradition for all Russian cosmonauts (at least, the male ones) ever since.

VOSTOK 1 blasted off into space on 12 April 1961.

Uh... it's a bit of a squeeze!

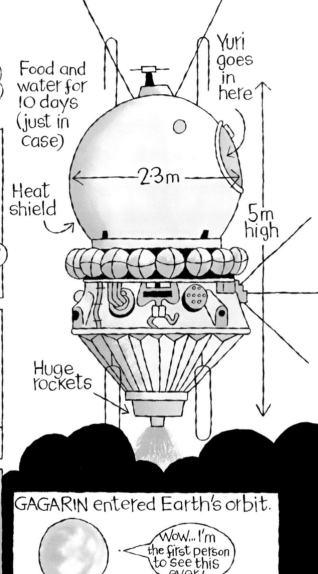

Food and water for 10 days (just in case)

Yuri goes in here

2·3 m

Heat shield

5m high

Huge rockets

GAGARIN entered Earth's orbit.

Wow... I'm the first person to see this ever!

Vostok 1 travelled at over 27000 km/h, flying around the Earth in 89 mins 34 secs.

The Americans were more determined than ever to win the next leg of the space race...

GRAVITY isn't as strong on the Moon as it is on Earth...

Wheee!

BUZZ ALDRIN was the second Moonwalker in the crew.

The astronauts took samples of lunar rock and dust, made notes and took photographs.

The American flag was planted on the Moon – it had to have a telescopic arm to make it fly without any wind.

Woof!

The landing was broadcast on TV – 500 million people watched.

There were 5 more Apollo missions and 10 more American astronauts walked on the Moon.

And because space was a brand new destination, people were desperate to do things FIRST...

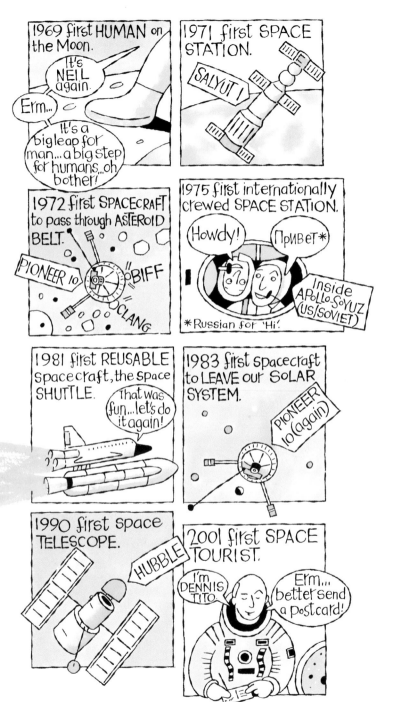

Meanwhile, amazing discoveries were still being made...

Meanwhile, we sent animals... we sent people... What could we send into space now?

SPACE PROBES

Sending PEOPLE into space is an awful lot of hassle.

You're telling ME!

SPACE PROBES are less bother. They don't get homesick and it doesn't matter if they're destroyed once they've finished their mission.

Tzzzt!

Tzzz

The first ones were sent to the Moon...

beepa beepa

This side is never seen from Earth

LUNA 3 gave us the first pictures of the far side of the Moon.

and Venus.

CCCP

Some space probes fly past planets and send images back to Earth.

Dear Earth, Having a lovely time in space. Wish you were here.
Mariner 9
X

Oooh, look at that!

The Solar and Heliospheric Observatory (SOHO) has been observing the Sun since 1996.

MARS EXPLORATION ROVERS, Spirit and Opportunity, landed on Mars in 2004.

beepa beepa

and they're still sending us information.

PHOENIX is the most recent visitor to Mars.

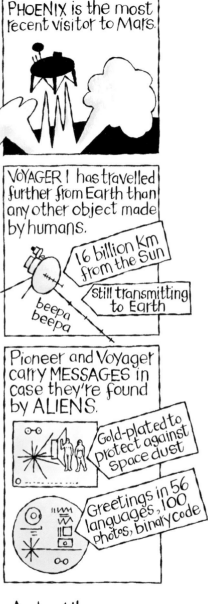

VOYAGER 1 has travelled further from Earth than any other object made by humans.

16 billion km from the Sun

still transmitting to Earth

beepa beepa

Some space probes leave our Solar System and sail away into distant space.

No, shy!

Hang on, what's that?

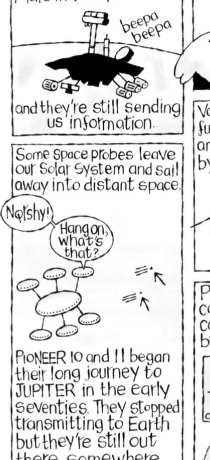

PIONEER 10 and 11 began their long journey to JUPITER in the early seventies. They stopped transmitting to Earth but they're still out there somewhere.

Pioneer and Voyager carry MESSAGES in case they're found by ALIENS.

Gold-plated to protect against space dust

Greetings in 56 languages, 100 photos, binary code

In 1974, a radio message with information about humans was sent into space, beamed at a cluster of stars called M13.

YAWN

But it's so far away we'll have to wait about 50,000 years for a reply.

drum drum

And until we get one...

75

SPACE STATIONS

In 1971, the USSR launched the first ever space station.

SALYUT 1

We've been up here for ages.

In the 1970s and 80s, there was a series of new, improved SALYUTS.

Longer than the Americans!

Meanwhile, the USA launched its own space station.

SKYLAB (USA)

But...

How are we going to take people there and back?

Err, the SPACE SHUTTLE won't be ready until 1981!

NASA

So Skylab was abandoned in 1974. In 1979 it fell to Earth in Australia ... killing a cow.

urk

The USA decided to build a reusable aircraft instead of more space stations.

But what if you actually LIVED there?

Exercising...

Astronauts on the first space stations came back to Earth very weak because there's no gravity to push against.

So we do lots of this to keep fit!

Going to the toilet...

Working...

Just off to do a few repairs...

in the terrifying emptiness of space.

Washing...

We try to avoid it as much as possible actually.

NASTY NIFF

And passing the time...

Floating tiddlywinks, anyone?

Not again!

Bet I can stay upside down the longest!

So, what's next?

How can humans explore other planets in our solar system?

A manned mission to MARS is planned within the next 20 years or so.

But it's going to be tricky!

We don't know how we'll cope with radiation.

And someone's got to think of a really good first line...

Er... One huge hop??

How can we travel OUTSIDE our solar system?

Ooh, now you're asking!

The speed limit of the Universe – the SPEED of LIGHT* – means that it would take an awfully long time to cross the vast distances of space.

Earth — more than 4 YEARS → our closest star

*And we can't get anywhere near that speed anyway.

But what about black holes? Could they be used to travel across the Universe?

ENTER here

WORM HOLES from one bit of space to another.

Ooh, ooh, where am I??

POP OUT over here

≡WHOOOSH≡

We know what will happen on planet Earth in billions of years...

SUN

Earth

But will humans still be here?

Maybe we'll be able to recreate Earth conditions on other planets?

But what will happen to the rest of the Universe in the future?

Brr...

The Universe will spread out endlessly and get cooler - the BIG CHILL.

crunch

OR the gravitational effect of all the matter in the Universe will be enough to reverse its expansion - the BIG CRUNCH.

But the expansion of the Universe is getting FASTER, because of DARK ENERGY!

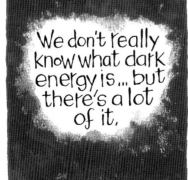

We don't really know what dark energy is... but there's a lot of it.

Maybe, if dark energy continues to get stronger, everything will pull apart...

The BIG RIP!

and BEYOND...

Will we ever make contact with intelligent life on other planets?

All over the world, people are listening...

to the furthest reaches of space...

beepa beepa

bleep bleep

tweeta tweet

cheep cheep

blip blop

beep

We're the SETI organisation...

the SEARCH for EXTRATERRESTRIAL INTELLIGENCE.

Yes!

We're listening for radio signals transmitted by ALIEN technology.

Perhaps one day we'll meet some...

Or perhaps, given the vastness of space and time, we never shall.

Tracey Turner

Tracey Turner writes books for children and adults about lots of different subjects, including famous writers, rude words, mysterious sliding rocks and, of course, the entire history of the Universe. When she's not travelling through space, she lives in Bath with Tom and their son, Toby.

Sally Kindberg

Sally Kindberg is an illustrator and writer. She once went to Elf School in Iceland, has written a book about hair, sailed on a tall ship to Lisbon and drawn the history of the world. She has one daughter, Emerald, and lives in London with 71 robots (and a couple of Moon rockets).

www.sallykindberg.co.uk

And for more Comic Strip History genius, don't miss ...